CHARADE

A Comedy in One Act

by

PHILIP JOHNSON

SAMUEL FRENCH

LONDON

NEW YORK TORONTO SYDNEY HOLLYWOOD

FOR AMATEUR PRODUCTION ENQUIRIES

UNITED KINGDOM AND WORLD
EXCLUDING NORTH AMERICA
plays@samuelfrench.co.uk
020 7255 4302/01

Each title is subject to availability from Samuel French, depending upon country of performance.

FOREWORD

THIS little comedy is a further development of what I always think of as the Lexham Gardens plays, the others being *Novelette, Hullabaloo* and *Matrimonial.* Upon completing the latter, I very arbitrarily decided that it was to be the last of the series, and was rash enough to announce the fact in a short foreword. Later, I had cause to regret this high-handedness : firstly, on account of the undoubted popularity of the plays ; secondly, because of Cook, Iris and Ivy themselves, whose feminine resentment at being thrust aside threatened to destroy the little peace of mind that I possess. They wheedled, they pestered, and they nagged. In the end, like a sensible fellow, I gave in, and here is *Charade.* Upon the slightest provocation, there will probably be several more.

PHILIP JOHNSON.

CHARACTERS

JANET COLYNGHAM.
ROSA ROSARIO.
COOK.
IRIS.
IVY.
MRS. LOCKETT.

The Play happens in the servants' room of a house in Lexham Gardens, Kensington, on an afternoon in Summer.

(All stage directions are given from the point of view of the audience.)

CHARADE

The Scene *is a room in the basement of a house in Lexham Gardens.*

The lady of the house, prompted by a praise-worthy, humanitarian instinct, has rebelled at the idea of the lives of her domestic staff being eternally bound by the four walls of a hot and airless kitchen, and she has therefore set aside this little domain for their rest and refreshment during their leisure hours. It is known as the servants' sitting-room. Facing it, there is a window in the centre of the back wall; a fireplace L.C., *and above this a door which leads to the kitchen. Another door in the back wall,* R. *of the window, admits one to the area. The walls of the room are covered with nondescript paper, and its furnishing is simple. In the centre is a square table, with straight-back chairs to* L., R. *and back of it. Beneath the window is a smaller table, and on this a fern. By the fireplace, slightly up stage, is an easy chair, and against the* R. *wall is a sofa. Both have seen better days. Below the fireplace is a faded cretonne-covered pouffe. Against the* R. *wall, below the sofa, is a wireless-cabinet. A small clock stands in the centre of the mantelpiece, flanked on either side by " ornaments." The themes of the few pictures have apparently been inspired by the major passions of love and war : men and maidens lingering by the old trysting-place, share the wall-space with scenes of carnage on the cavalry battlefield. There are, too, a few colourful trades-men's calendars, and, up* R., *a small wall-mirror. Upon the larger table are a few magazines of the " Woman's Weekly " type.*

It is the early afternoon of a summer's day. Cook, *looking extremely hot and red in the face, is seated on the sofa, fanning herself with a newspaper. A cup of tea is beside her on the sofa. She is middle-aged,*

*inclined to stoutness and would be God's gift to an
artist seeking a model for any of those advertisements
extolling the domestic Nirvana to be attained through
using So-and-So's Soap Flakes, or Thingummy's
Meat Cubes. IVY, the kitchenmaid, is seated on the
chair L. of the table, also drinking a cup of tea. She
is a nondescript young girl, of about sixteen, who of
late has developed some rather hoydenish traits, and
who lives in a state of perpetual variance with her
stockings, always on the point of coming down.*

COOK (*after a gusty sigh*). Why it should be, Ivy,
I'm sure I know no more than the man in the moon,
but lamb cutlets get me down these days, and that's
a fact. (*She places the newspaper on the sofa—takes
up the cup of tea.*) A sole Mornay, now, or a lobster
cream, or very near anything you like to mention, I
seem to just take in my stride. (*She takes a sip of
tea.*) But when Madam said to me this morning,
"Cutlets for lunch to-day, Cook," her words seemed
to strike on my ears like a death-knell. I had to fair
force myself to cook 'em, and now it's all over, I feel
like a drooping lily or a broken doll—yes, I do!
IVY. You don't look much like either, do you,
Cook?
COOK (*who does not appear to have caught the words*).
Eh? (*She takes another sip of tea.*) I was telling the
landlady of "The Pembroke Arms" about it only the
other night—I'd just slipped in to dodge a shower, on
account of my best hat—and I said to her, "Don't
mention the name of cutlets to me, for I cannot abide
the nasty things." And what d'you think she said?
IVY. Er—"Same again?"
COOK. No, she did not, Miss Saucy! And what's
more, she's a very ladylike lady, I'll have you know.
Dresses very quiet in black satin, and if ever I *did*
break my rule and take a second glass she'd say, "A
little of something similar, dear?" or "Shall I
repeat?"
IVY. But what did she say about the cutlets,
Cook?

Cook. She said she'd once read all about that sort of thing in a book, and it meant that my mother was frightened by a sheep before I was born. . . . Of course, there may be something in it. You never know. (*She takes another sip of tea.*) Phoo! but this here tea's making me hotter than ever, drat it!

Ivy. I've nearly finished mine. (*Tipping her head back, she drinks the last of her tea, somewhat noisily, then displays the empty cup.*) Look! It's quite empty now!

Cook (*grimly*). I don't have to look—I heard! Just for a minute I thought the kitchen-geyser had sprung a leak.

Ivy. But—but you are going to do my fortune for me, aren't you, Cook, like you said?

Cook. I'm not so sure if I can. I mayn't be in the right mood.

Ivy. Oh, but, Cook, you promised! You know you did! You did Iris's yesterday, and you said you'd do me mine to-day! Oh, *Cook*!

Cook. Iris's teacup's always easy. There's never anything in it but soldiers. Yesterday, it was a red-haired guardsman, and even then, if you please, she wasn't satisfied. Oh dear, no! She'd got a new emerald-green costume, so couldn't he be on the dark side, instead of red? "Iris," I said, "I cannot tamper or play fast and loose with Fate. I'm only telling you what I see in the tea-leaves, and this here man's got hair the colour of tomato-soup—and if you don't like it, you can lump it!"

Ivy. But—but you don't *really* see things, do you, Cook?

Cook (*sharply*). What d'you mean? D'you think I make it all up out of my head or something? Eh?

Ivy (*hastily*). No, no, of course you don't! I think you're awful clever at it, Cook—I do, reely! And—and you will do me mine, Cook, won't you?— Oh, but, *please*!

Cook. I've told you once, I mayn't be in the mood. Them cutlets have put me all nohow.

IVY. Oh, but, Cook——

COOK. Oh, all right! all right! you little pest!
But don't go blaming me if I see something nasty in
it, that's all.

IVY. Oh, thank you, Cook!

COOK. Tip your cup upside-down, and then turn
it towards you three times, like as if you're stirring a
pudding, and then lay it down in the saucer. Go on!

IVY (*obeying these directions*). Like this?

COOK. That's right. Leave it upside-down in the
saucer for a minute—and while we're waiting for it to
work, you can just slip into the kitchen and give
Trixie a saucer of milk.

IVY. She's had two already.

COOK. Do as you're told, will you, and don't
argue! She's looking depressed to-day.

IVY. Oh, all right.

(*She rises and goes off through the open doorway and
into the kitchen. The moment she is alone,* COOK'S
*manner becomes tinged with a certain furtiveness.
Shifting her cup and saucer from her right hand to
her left, she thrusts the former down behind the
upholstery at the back of the sofa. Not immediately
finding what she seeks, her expression registers
anxiety, and she mutters unintelligibly to herself.
The next moment, however, her fingers close upon the
object of her search, and her expression changes
swiftly to one of relief, as she draws forth a black
bottle. Hastily setting the cup and saucer beside her
on the sofa, she uncorks the bottle and pours a little
nip into her tea. She is in the act of recorking the
bottle when there is a slight sound from the direction
of the kitchen.* COOK *thrusts the bottle behind the
sofa cushion, as* MRS. LOCKETT, *the charwoman,
enters. She is a drab, frail-looking little woman of
about sixty. Upon her head, skewered to her scanty
hair by a hat-pin, is a battered relic which once upon
a time was a man's cap, and over her draggled, shape-
less clothes she wears a rough-apron.*)

MRS. LOCKETT (*timidly—hesitantly*). If you please,

Missis Gosling, I see as there's a scrap of cold pudding set by as though maybe to be thrown away, and I was wondering if—if——

Cook (*with a little gesture—magnanimously*). That's quite all right, Mrs. Lockett. You take it home with you. I'll give you a bit of paper for it before you go.

Mrs. Lockett. Oh, thank you kindly, Missis Gosling. I'm humbly grateful. I wouldn't ask for myself, but our Sally 'as took quite a fancy to cold pudding, and if you're quite sure as 'er upstairs won't mind . . .

Cook. Her upstairs won't get the chance. My motto is the same as any other cook's that's worth her salt : what the eye can't see, the heart won't grieve over, and if a hair-pin falls in the batter, why, fish it out, and who's to know ? You take the pudding home to your Sally, and welcome.

Mrs. Lockett. I'm sure as I'm greatly obliged. (*She gives a little sigh and a shake of the head.*) It's few enough treats she gets these days, our Sally. (*She turns to go.*)

Cook. And how's Mr. Lockett keeping ? As per usual, eh ?

Mrs. Lockett. Well, 'e's off it just at present, thank you ; been off it for over a week, in a manner of speaking—though of course there's no knowing when 'e'll be on it again. 'E's a variable man, is Lockett, and no mistake.

Cook (*taking up her cup and saucer*). It's a terrible, terrible thing, the drink ! (*She takes a sip of her tea, with very evident satisfaction.*) Oh, terrible !

Mrs. Lockett. And no one more against it than Lockett, mind you, when 'e 'appens to be off it. Oh, awful against it 'e is, calling it all the diabolical names as 'e can lay 'is tongue to, and off to temp'rance meetings most every night. In fact, it's usually the temp'rance meetings what starts 'im off again.

Cook. No !

Mrs. Lockett. They preaches that powerful over what 'appens to them as gives way to it, it brings 'im out all of a lather, to think what a narrow squeak

'e's 'ad, and 'e 'as to call at " The Pig and Whistle "
on 'is way 'ome to pull 'imself round—and before 'e
rightly knows where 'e is, why, there 'e is—on it
again !

COOK (*clicking her tongue sympathetically*). Tck !
Tck ! Tck !

MRS. LOCKETT. Still, 'e weren't so bad the last
time. Leastways, 'e didn't 'ave the 'orrors, not
properly.

COOK. No pink snakes, or nothing ?

MRS. LOCKETT. It never 'as been snakes, with
Lockett : it's always little green pianners what keep
opening their lids and snapping at 'im—and last time
it weren't even them. And never a wrong word for
our Sally, and only blacked *one* of me eyes, and even
then 'e seemed sort of 'alf-'earted about it. . . . I
felt quite worried, in a way. I wouldn't like to think
as 'e were breaking up, if you know what I mean.
(*Turning to go.*) Eh, well, I'll be getting on with me
brasses. And thank you kindly for the cold pudding.
Our Sally won't 'alf wag 'er tail and bark when she
sees it !

(*She goes out, nearly colliding with* IVY *in the doorway.*)

IVY (*boisterously—as she enters*). Trixie's had her
milk, and she's been sick, and you're going to do my
fortune for me now, aren't you, Cook ?

COOK. Oh, am I never to know the blessing of a
moment's peace ?

IVY. Oh, but, Cook——

COOK. That'll do, now ! Pull your stockings up
and stop that whining, for goodness' sake, do !

(IVY *drags impatiently at her stockings.* COOK *drains
her cup, then rises.*)

If it's my fate to wear myself to a thread for others,
so be it ! (*Going to behind the table—placing her cup
and saucer on the table.*) Here, give me your cup, and
let's get it over !

IVY (*snatching up her cup—thrusting it into* COOK's
hand—excitedly). Here you are, Cook, here you are !

(*Clasping her hands and hopping up and down in her excitement.*) Oooh! Oooh! but I wonder what you'll see!

(COOK *peers frowningly into the cup for a moment, then gives a dramatic start.*)

COOK. Ha! I knew it! I *knew* it! That chocolate mould you said the cat had took! And here you are, Miss, here you are, wolfing it yourself behind the larder-door, as large as life!—*Well*, of all the dirty little story-tellers! And to lay it on to a poor innocent animal that can't speak up for itself! Ivy Parker, you should be ashamed!

IVY (*her enthusiasm considerably dashed*). Oh, Cook——

COOK. Hold your tongue, will you, and let me see what else I can find! (*Peering into the cup.*) Mmmmm! My word, but there's trouble here, if you like! Oh, yes! Here's you crying your eyes out, and Madam packing you off at a minute's notice, for not getting up the first time you're called of a morning!

IVY. Is there—is there nothing about me acting in a pantomime, and wearing tights?

COOK. There's some perfectly horrible things in this cup, Ivy, but nothing so horrible as the idea of you in tights.

IVY. I did so want to act in a pantomime, Cook! It's my secret ambition! It is, reely!

COOK (*bluntly*). The tea-leaves say No—so that's that!

IVY. Oh, *Cook*!

COOK. And you needn't keep saying " Oh, Cook," neither. This is Fate, and you can't get away from it! (*Peering again into the cup.*) Here, wait a minute, though, what's this? . . . There's something here that looks to me like a horseshoe!

IVY (*reviving somewhat*). Oooh! That means good luck for me, doesn't it, Cook? Eh? That's good luck, isn't it? Oooh!

(IRIS, *unnoticed by either, enters.*)

Cook. Don't you be so grasping! It mayn't be for you at all. (*Twisting the cup this way and that as she studies the tea-leaves.*) Now, this is what I call interesting, for there's a message here that's as plain as the nose on your face! It says—an opportunity is about to arise, which, if made proper use of, will bring fame and fortune to someone in this house! There, now!

Iris. And for once in your life, Cook, you and your tea-leaves are *right*!

Cook (*turning quickly—with a little start*). Eh?— *Iris*! Iris, I'll thank you not to come creeping in on me when I'm concentrating! It's a shock to my system, it is!

Iris. Oh, yeah?

(Iris, *the parlourmaid, is quite pretty, has a neat figure, and is very, very sure of herself. She is at the moment in an obvious state of ill-suppressed excitement.*)

Cook. And I want none of your impudence, neither! And why aren't you changed? It's your afternoon out, isn't it?

Iris. I'm staying in.

Cook. But I thought you was going to Kew Gardens with a Royal Horse Guard.

Iris. I've changed my mind. He can take his horse instead.

Cook. Ho?

Iris. That fame and fortune you saw just now— it's just round the corner, waiting to be grabbed— and *I'm* going to grab it! (*a descriptive gesture.*) Like this!

Ivy (*clamorously*). But you can't! It's mine. It's in my tea-cup! (*She tries to snatch the cup.*) Oh, *Cook*!

Cook (*slapping her hand*). Be quiet, Ivy, will you!

Iris (*her excitement increasing—breathlessly*). This is a red-letter day for me, all right! All I've got to do is to play my cards right, and this afternoon sees

the turning-point in my whole career! You wait,
Cook, just you wait!

COOK (*putting the cup down on the table*). Iris,
what's come over you?

IRIS. Many's the time my Auntie Gladys has said
to me, "Iris, you're not just a fool: you're a damn'
fool! You, with your face and figure, to be hiding
yourself away in service! It's a sin and a shame,
and I don't know what you're thinking of."—But
that's all over now, Cook! My chance has come at
last! At *last*!

COOK. What d'you mean?

IRIS (*hurrying to* R., *to the small mirror*). I'm going
on the films, that's what!

COOK. You're—— (*A step nearer to her.*) Look
here, have you been at the cooking-sherry, or what?

IRIS (*prinking her hair in the mirror*). Cooking-
sherry, indeed! Why, this time next year I'll be
bathing in champagne! You see if I'm not! (*Turning from the mirror—snapping her fingers.*) So *that*
to your cooking-sherry!

COOK. Of course, you may know what you're
talking about——

IRIS. I've told you—I'm going on the films—and
what's more, you're going to help me there!

COOK (*staring at her*). Eh?

IRIS. I've planned it all out—up in my room, just
now—and, oh, Cook, it really is my chance at last—
and you will help me, won't you?—you won't let me
down?

COOK (*raising her voice*). You're tempting me very
strong indeed, Iris Warburton, to *knock* you down, so
there!

IRIS. And I'm not going to be Iris Warburton any
more, either! I've thought out a lovely new name
for myself—Melody Dawne! What d'you think of
that for a glamour-name, eh? Melody Dawne!

COOK. Don't ask me! You've got me that tied
up, I can hardly remember my own name, now.

IVY. It's Martha Gosling! And that fame and
fortune was in my cup, wasn't it, Cook?

IRIS. Oh, shut up, you little squib !

IVY (*shouting*). But it was ! It was ! It was !

COOK (*to her*). See : if you don't pipe down this very instant-minute, I'll shake you till your teeth fall out, I will !

IVY. You can't, then ! Mine aren't like yours— they're fastened to me !

COOK (*very incensed*). Ho, indeed ! Then it's a pity your stockings aren't fastened to you, too ! Talk about concertinas ! Just look at 'em !

IVY (*dragging at her stockings*). Oh !

COOK. And as for you, Iris, just you calm your- self, and tell me what all this hue and cry's about.

IRIS. I keep telling you, don't I ?—I'm going on the films !—and it's all through the lady that's been lunching with Madam to-day—Miss Rosa Rosario, the famous woman film-producer !

COOK. Never heard of her.

IRIS. And she's just waiting to start on a lovely new film, and she was going on to Madam about it all through lunch, and I couldn't help hearing.

COOK. I know how hard you tried not to ! I know !

IRIS. No, Cook, listen ! Listen to this, because this is the bit where I come in ! " Here we are, all ready to begin," she said to Madam, " and everything held up on account of one part. Quite a small part," she said, " but very important. And it's *got* to be the right type. We've combed London from end to end," she said, " and so far we haven't found a single actress who comes within a mile of it."

IVY. Would the lady who acts it have to wear tights ?

COOK (*with an impatient gesture*). Tsst !

IRIS. And then—and then, Cook, she said this : " We're so desperate, Janet," she said, " that if we could find someone who'd never acted before, but who was *right* for the part, we'd take her and train her for it." There, now !

COOK. Oh ?

IRIS. And a bit later, I caught her looking at me

sort of sideways, and I heard her whisper to Madam, "What an extremely pretty girl." (*She pauses for* Cook *to make some remark, but* Cook *does not oblige.*) Meaning me, Cook.

Cook (*with a shrug*). Oh, well, there's no accounting for taste. I once knew a man called his bulldog "Beauty."

Iris. So you see!

Cook. See what?

Iris. Why, it's my chance, of course!

Cook. Oh?

Iris. But of course it is! Oh, Cook, don't be so dense! Don't you see? When this Miss Rosario sees me acting, she'll know her search is ended, and she'll give me the part at once! I don't mind if it is only a small part, just to begin. You wait till a year from now! Melody Dawne! That'll be me!

Cook. But, Iris, even film stars must have to act a bit sometimes, and you can't.

Iris. That's all you know. I've been practising for weeks and weeks in my bedroom, Cook, and I act beautifully! I do, really! Listen to this! (*Moving a few paces away—halting—flinging her arms out wide —reciting with terrific dramatic emphasis.*) "The quality of mercy is not strained! It droppeth as the gentle rain from—(*she pauses—raising her right arm— pointing to the ceiling*) Heaven, upon the earth (*she pauses—thrusting her left arm downwards—pointing to the floor*) beneath!"—There! What d'you think of that?

(Ivy *splutters with laughter.*)

Cook. Well, Iris, since you ask me—— (*She breaks off. To* Ivy.) Ivy!!!

(Ivy *covers her mouth with her hand.*)

Since you ask me, I can only say that even if nothing else comes of it, the exercise should do you good. Much more of that there arm business, and you'll have muscles on you like a cart-horse.

Iris (*impatiently—going again to the mirror*). **Oh,** what d'you know about acting, anyway ?

Cook. Nothing at all, dear. I'm surprised at you wasting your talent on me.—But this I will say, Iris Warburton, if you're an actress, then I'm a beautiful bird of paradise !

Iris (*studying her reflection*). All *right* ! You wait till Miss Rosario sees me, that's all. She'll think very different.

Cook. And where, pray, is she going to see you ?

Iris. Here, in this room, of course.

Cook. Eh ?

Iris. Madam's going to show her all over the house, this afternoon. I heard her say so. (*Turning swiftly from the mirror—going to* Cook.) Oh, Cook— it's my chance—and you will help me, won't you ?— I've got it all planned out beautifully—oh, Cook, *please* !

Cook. But, what d'you expect me to do ?

Iris. Just act a little scene with me, that's all—so she can see at a glance how talented I am. Oh, you will, won't you ?

Cook (*staring at her*). Iris . . . have you any idea what you're talking about ?

Iris. Don't you see ? When they come into this room, they'll find you and me acting this little scene— only they won't know it's acting—they'll think it's real—and then, when we tell them it was acting, Miss Rosario will say " What a clever, clever girl ! " and she'll offer me the part straight off, and this time next year I'll be Melody Dawne, with my name in lights, and the world at my feet, and the sound of thousands cheering in my ears !

Cook. And you'll wake up and find it's the alarm-clock, and it's Monday morning, and raining like stink ! I know !

Iris. Oh, Cook !

Cook. Now, listen to me, Iris : you put on your hat and go off to Kew with that Horse Guard. A little fresh air may do you good. (*She goes to* L. *by the fireplace.*)

IRIS (*shaking her head*). I've done with all that sort of thing. All that matters to me now is my career ! And what's more, you should be pleased to see me so ambitious and not go trying to discourage me.

COOK. Then why can't you be ambitious in your own line ? Stick to your proper job, and who knows but one day you might rise to be a cook—like me !

IRIS (*disdainfully*). Thanks very much.

COOK. And you needn't look down your nose at cooks, neither ! They're more important than film stars any day. You can give a man all the glamour in creation—and then watch him leave it for a good square meal ! I'm a woman of the world, and I know !

IVY. Cook——

IRIS. You seem to think nothing matters but food. Food !

COOK. And I'm not far wrong. You try doing without it for a week.

IVY. Cook—the young gentleman what brings the vegetables says I've got glamour, he does !

IRIS. My God !

COOK. Then he must be greener even than his own lettuces ! (*She takes her work-bag from the easy chair.*)

IVY. He isn't, then ! He's very clever, and goes to college at a night school, and he's taught me how to say " Thank you " in French !

COOK. If I ever heard you say it in English, I'd drop down dead with surprise ! (*She sits in the easy chair.*)

IRIS. Oh, Cook, do stop bothering with her !

(*As* COOK *takes her knitting from her bag.*)

And don't start knitting, neither. Miss Rosario and Madam may be here any minute now, and we haven't arranged our scene !

COOK. Iris, don't tell me you're serious, for I can't believe it.

IRIS. But I am, Cook, I am ! Here's my chance of a part on the films, and I'm not going to let it

slip! I don't care how small it is! You've got to
start from the bottom in everything, haven't you?

Ivy. Divers don't, do they, Cook?

Cook. Ivy!! (*To* Iris.) If you're set on making
a fool of yourself, Iris, all right—but don't drag me
into it, is all I ask.

Iris. But I can't act a scene on my own, can I?

Cook (*commencing to knit*). That's your look-out.

Iris (*pleadingly*). Oh, Cook, you can't say No!

Cook. It was the first word my mother taught me.
And will you not chatter while I'm knitting. This
here moss-rose pattern wants all my attention—so
kindly shut up!

(Iris *is silent for a moment obviously debating something
in her mind. She looks calculatingly at* Cook, *then
ventures a little nearer to her.*)

Iris (*in a smooth, wheedling voice*). Cook . . .
listen . . . if you'll do as I ask, I'll . . . I'll buy you
that dressy blouse you saw in Pontings window.
There!

Cook (*ceasing to knit for a moment—then resuming
with increased speed*). No, Iris—when my mind is
made up, it's made up—and no one shall say I
abandoned my principles for the sake of a dressy
blouse.

Iris (*not entirely discouraged—still in the same
voice*). You'd look ever so smart and classy in it,
Cook, you know you would.

Cook. That's as maybe.

Iris. That there waterfall of lace down the front
is just your style to a T, isn't it?

Cook (*still knitting*). M'm?

Iris. Real lady-like. You do know the one I
mean, don't you, Cook?

Cook (*counting stitches*). One—two—three—four
. . . There was a string of beads laid across it, care-
lessly-like, wasn't there?

Iris. That's the one! The moment I set eyes on
it, I said to myself, " That's the very blouse for
Cook! "

COOK (*counting more stitches*). Five—six—seven—eight . . . I remember thinking how the blouse and the beads seemed to set each other off, somehow. It quite struck me.

IRIS (*after a moment's hesitation—giving in*). All right, then, Cook—all right, you do as I ask, and you shall have the beads as well—and I can't say fairer, now can I ?

(COOK *immediately starts to fold her knitting.*)

Oh, Cook—you will ?

COOK. In the sacred cause of friendship, and for no other reason, Iris, I'll do my best for you. (*Stuffing her knitting into her bag.*) And if you slip along to Pontings straight after tea, you'll just about get there before they shut—and if you dare to come back without that dressy blouse *and* beads, God help you ! (*Rising.*) If I'm to be bribed and corrupted, so be it—but I'll see it's done proper. (*Tossing her bag on to the table.*) And now, what's all this nonsense about, eh ? What d'you want me to do ?

IRIS. I've told you—just act this little scene with me, so Miss Rosario can see how talented I am.

COOK. But I can't act—and I've sense enough to know it, what's more.

IRIS. That won't matter : they'll be looking at me, not you.

COOK. Oh, they will, will they ? Well, supposing that's just where you're wrong, and this Miss What's-her-name gets struck all of a heap over me, and picks on me for her film, eh ?

IRIS (*who clearly considers this beyond the wildest realms of possibility*). We'll just have to risk it, that's all.

COOK. H'm ! And what's this thing we're to act, anyway ? It's got to be nothing suggestive, mind, or I'll have no truck with it, so there !

IRIS. Oh, don't be silly !

IVY (*bursting in on the conversation*). I once saw a play, I did, and it was lovely ! All about a lady what's married to a handsome gentleman named

Archibald, and they've got a little nipper named Willie, and——

Iris. Oh, Ivy, be quiet, while Cook and me decide what we're to do !

Ivy. No, but I want to tell you !

Cook. Ivy ! ! That will *do* ! ! !

Ivy (*refusing to be daunted*). And she goes off and leaves her husband, through the neighbours making trouble, and he thinks she's dead, see ? and after a bit he goes and marries another lady, and——

Iris. Oh, Ivy, will you stop it !

Ivy (*determined to be heard—slightly louder—while* Cook *and* Iris *exchange despairing looks*). And then the lady what's Willie's ma comes back to Archibald, and when she finds he's all hooked up with another lady, she isn't half in a stew about it, and carries on something alarming, and after a bit she quietens down and says : " It's all my fault, what a pity," and she doesn't let on to Archibald who she is, see ? and he doesn't know her from Adam because she's wearing blue glasses, and it's all ever so sad, and she gets herself taken on as nurse to Willie, him what's her own nipper, and he's took ill and dies, and she screeches out, " Gor blimey, he's conked out and never called me Mum," and then she dies too, and I cried ever so, I did, and it was lovely, and I dreamt about Archibald every night for a week, he was that handsome !

Cook. Have you quite finished, Ivy ?

(Ivy, *quite out of breath, nods.*)

You've nothing more to say ?

(Ivy *shakes her head.*)

Thank you. Then perhaps me and Iris can get on with the job. (*To* Iris.) Now, Iris, what's this here scene to be about ? After all, it's got to be about something, I suppose.

Iris. We shall just make it up as we go along, don't you see ? All we want is the right idea, just to start us off !

Cook. Is that all ? I see.

Iris. Only there's got to be lots of emotion in it, so she can see how good I am at it. You know——something where I'm all laughing one minute, and crying the next, because that's real Art, that is!

Cook. Let's hope she doesn't mistake it for gin!

Iris. Oh, Cook, we've got to be serious—here's me with my whole career at stake! Can't you think of *anything* ? What we want is what they call a short dramatic situation—if you know what a dramatic situation is.

Cook (*with a nod*). Like when your petticoat comes down in the street. I know.

Iris. But it's got to be a sort of little story, Cook, don't you see ? Something that's sad at first, and then ends all happy, so that I can be emotional.

Cook (*after a moment—with sudden inspiration*). I know! I've got it, Iris! I've got the very thing! What about us acting that I'm the lady of the house, and you're the charwoman——

Iris (*coldly*). What ?

Cook. Wait a minute! And I give you the sack, see ? And you're all cut up about it, because you've got a husband with only one leg and six children, and you crawl up to me on your hands and knees, and beg and implore me to take you on again, but I'm not having any and I say, " No, you slut ! " and kick you ; and you do a lot more begging and imploring, and I kick you again, but in the end I say, " Oh, all right, just this once, but never again," and then of course you're happy and kiss my hand all over !—There, now ! What d'you think of that, eh ?

Iris. Nothing at all. It's awful.

Cook. Oh, well, Iris, if you can think of a better.

Iris. As a matter of fact, I have . . . Now—now listen to this very carefully, Cook. When Madam and Miss Rosario come into the room, they'll find me all upset—you know, crying and carrying on. And why ? Because—because I've just that minute had a letter to say that my fiancé has fallen into the Thames, and all is over!

Cook (*considering this*). I'd make it the Serpentine, Iris, if I was you. The Thames sounds so common, somehow.

Iris. Oh, all right, then. He was rowing in a boat on the Serpentine, see ?   And he fell in and was drowned.

Ivy. Why couldn't he swim ?

Iris. Because he couldn't, of course !

Ivy. What a namby-pamby ! When I get engaged, I bet my young man'll be able to swim like a duck, he will.

Iris. He'll have about as much brain as a duck, too, if he gets himself engaged to you.

Ivy. That's all you know, then ! You wait and see ! The vegetable gentleman says I was never meant to be a kitchenmaid.

Cook. Neither were the monkeys in the Zoo, so pull up your stockings and keep quiet !

Ivy. I don't care ! I——

Cook. *Ivy !* That will *do* ! (*To* Iris.) Go on, Iris.

Iris. Well, you try to comfort me, and that's where the sad part comes in, you see ?

Cook (*nodding*). Ah.

Iris. And then, when I've been sad enough for Miss Rosario to see how sad I can be when I try, we read the letter again, and find it's all a mistake. He isn't drowned at all—and then, and then, of course, I'm happy again.

Cook. I see.

Iris. Now, are you sure you can remember it, Cook ?   They come into the room and find me crying.

Cook. And I say, " What are you bawling your head off over now, eh ? "

Iris. No, you don't ! You say " What is amiss, my pretty one ? " You know, with a sort of throb in your voice.

Cook (*in rich, mellifluous tones*). " What is amiss, my pretty one ? "—Like that ?

(Ivy *splutters with laughter*.)

Ivy ! !

Ivy. You sounded as though you were gargling with treacle, Cook.

Iris. Oh, be quiet, Ivy, do! (*To* Cook.) It'll have to do. And after that, we just make up the rest ourselves.

Ivy. And what am I to be? What do I do, eh?

Iris. You? You just keep quiet, that's what you do!

Ivy. Well, I won't then! I want to act, too, and if I can't, I won't be quiet—so there!

Cook. Ivy!!!

Ivy (*wailing*). Oh, but, Cook, I want to act, and Iris won't let me. Oh, Cook! It isn't fair.

Cook (*a happy thought*). I tell you what, Ivy: you can be Iris's sister—the one that's deaf and dumb.

Ivy. Like this, d'you mean? (*She flops down on the pouffe, down* L., *and sits, very rigid, her arms straight down at her sides, and her mouth slightly open, staring fixedly in front of her.*)

Cook. That's lovely! You keep just like that all the time, and don't move, and maybe you'll get snapped up for the films, too!

Ivy (*springing up*). Oh, Cook!

Iris. Sssh! Hush!

(*They all listen.*)

Oh, my goodness, I thought I heard them coming! (*Taking the chair from* R. *of the table.*) See, Cook, we'll have this over here. (*She places it* R.C.) And you can be sitting on it. It'll look better than both of us standing. We shan't look so fixed-like—— Oh, and the letter!—the letter!—we'll have to have something for the letter!——

Ivy. There's that bit of paper on the mantel-piece.

Iris. That'll do! (*She darts across to* L. *and takes a piece of paper from the mantelpiece.*)

Cook (*with her eyes tightly shut—memorizing*). "What is amiss, my pretty one? What is amiss, my pretty one? What is amiss, my pretty one?"

Iris (*standing* L., *in a sudden rapture—her hands*

clasped ecstatically to her bosom). Oh, Cook!—isn't it wonderful, to think that, any minute now, I may be launched on my career! Melody Dawne! I can hardly believe it!

COOK (*opening her eyes for a moment*). Let's hope you're not counting your chickens before they're hatched, Iris, that's all. (*Shutting her eyes again.*) "What is amiss, my pretty one?"

IRIS. Of course I'm not. I've got a presentiment. —And you want to say that out loud, so they'll hear you properly.

(*There is a slight noise from the direction of the kitchen.*)

COOK. They're here! They're coming!—Oh!——
IRIS (*dashing across to R.*). Oh!—Ivy, sit down!— Cook!—Oh!——

(IVY *bounces on to the pouffe, and goes into her former attitude.* COOK *hastily seats herself on the chair* R.C., IRIS *stands just to* R. *of her. There is a further slight noise from the kitchen.*)

They're here! (*Hissing at* COOK—*agitatedly.*) Go on! Start! Start, can't you! "What is amiss ——"

COOK (*all fluttered and flurried*). Eh?
IRIS (*hissing at her again*). "What is amiss——" Go *on*!
COOK. Oh——

(*Raising her voice—as* MRS. LOCKETT *enters from the kitchen.*)

"What is amiss, my pretty one?"
MRS. LOCKETT (*who is carrying a pail of water—in her usual mild voice*). Nothing at all, Missis Gosling. I'm just going to swill the area-steps.
COOK (*confused*). Oh, yes—yes, that's right, Mrs. Lockett. H'm!
MRS. LOCKETT. Thank you, Missis Gosling.

(*Carrying her pail, she trails up stage to the area door, opens it and goes out, closing it behind her.*)

Iris (*impatiently*).   Oh, what did *she* want to come barging in for ?

Cook (*her hand pressed to her heart*).   Oh dear ! And just when I'd worked myself up to it, too !

Ivy (*relaxing her attitude*).   I wish I could act deaf and dumb and wear tights as well, I do.

Cook.   Really, Ivy, the way you keep harping on tights is nothing less than morbid.

Ivy.   Would the vegetable gentleman feel morbid if he saw me in tights ?

Cook.   Ivy ! ! !   That will *do* ! !   I'm sure I can't think where you get your ideas from, I can't, really !

Ivy.   The vegetable gentleman says I give him ideas, Cook.

Cook.   I'll give him more than ideas, if I catch him wasting your time, I will.

Ivy.   He doesn't like Iris at all.   He calls her " Stuck-up Tottie."   (*She giggles.*)

Iris.   *What* ?

Ivy.   But he likes you, Cook—he says he bets you're a proper old sport when you've had a couple.

Cook (*very indignantly*).   Ho ! he does, does he, the saucy upstart !   You wait till I see him !   I'll give him a piece of my mind he'll remember to his dying day, you see if I don't !   Had a couple, indeed ! The very idea !

(*During this latter speech, voices have been heard off stage—or rather, a voice, that of* Miss Rosario. *As* Iris's *ears catch the sound, she gives* Cook *a violent nudge.*)

And don't do *that*, Iris !   (*Suddenly realizing.*)   Eh ?

(*At this moment,* Janet Colyngham *and her friend* Rosa Rosario *enter.* Janet Colyngham, *the mistress of the house, is nearer fifty than forty, well groomed and quite attractive looking.   There is, how-ever, a somewhat strained and exhausted look about her this afternoon, the reason for which is very soon apparent.* Rosa Rosario, *who is perhaps a year or two younger, is a very tailor-made looking person, wearing tweeds and horn-rimmed spectacles.   But, alas, it is not the eye which the lady engages, so much as the ear; for* ROSA *is a " Talker," and, moreover, a " Talker " with a one-track mind: one of those beings whose torrent of words has the quality of sapping the listener's brain, leaving it limp, helpless, and whimpering for aspirin. Needless to say, she is talking rapidly as she enters.)*

ROSA. "The whole *thing*," as I said to Monty only last Tuesday—or it may have been Wednesday— " The whole *thing*," as I said, " is a question of *type* ! Give me the *type*," I said, " and I'll give you your film ! But I cannot make bricks without straw, and you must not expect me to ! And it's no use coming to me with a long face, Monty darling," I said, " and telling me that the delay's costing two hundred pounds a day ! I don't care if it's costing two thousand ! I don't care " (*snapping her fingers*) " that much. No, no, no," I said, " not one inch of film will I shoot, until my artistic sense tells me that I've got the right woman for the part, the right *type* ! "— You do see what I mean, Janet dear, don't you ? The utterly, utterly, utterly right *type* !

JANET (*wearily*). Yes, dear, of course. Er—this is——

ROSA. I've combed the whole of London, literally *combed* it, and I'm prepared to comb the whole of England, too. Of course, the country's stiff with women who are aching to go on the films, God knows why ! Stiff with them ! Oh, I know ! I know ! Their letters lie on my desk like a snowdrift ! But what use are they to me, if they're not the right *type* ? Fat, thin, short, or tall, they might just as well be at the bottom of the sea. As I said to Monty, " If they're the *wrong* type," I said " don't waste my time with them, *please* ! "—You do follow me, Janet, don't you ?

JANET. Oh, quite. (*Louder.*) Er—this, Rosa, is the servants' room.

ROSA (*not even glancing round*). Yes, yes, dear, very nice.

(Since the entrance of the dynamic and voluble ROSA, *neither* COOK *nor* IRIS *has moved.* IVY, *of course, is still on the pouffe. It is clear that, before this spate of words, their plan has crumbled away as surely as a child's sand-castle before an oncoming tide. It is doubtful indeed if* ROSA *has been aware of their existence. At this point, however, she does become conscious of* IRIS.)

(Pointing to her.) Now—now, you take that girl over there, for instance. *(Her hand on* JANET'S *arm.)* You stay here, dear. *(Going to* IRIS.) You! What's your name?

IRIS *(staring at her as though mesmerized).* Er——

ROSA. Never mind. It doesn't matter. You want to go on the films, of course, don't you?

IRIS *(finding her voice—eagerly).* Oh, yes—yes, please, Miss Rosario, I——

ROSA *(to* JANET—*triumphantly).* You see? I knew it! Like all the rest, *she* wants to go on the films—and stands about as much chance as she does of flying to the moon!

IRIS *(with a gasp). What?*

ROSA *(grasping* IRIS'S *shoulders—twisting her round).* Take a look at her! Front! Side! Back! There you are! Goodish figure! Pretty! But in the same way that billions of other girls are pretty! Billions! She isn't just the *wrong* type! She's no type at all!

(Releasing IRIS *so suddenly that the latter staggers slightly.)*

Hopeless, of course! Perfectly hopeless!

IRIS *(weakly).* Oh, Miss Rosario, d'you mean I——

ROSA *(who has lost all interest in her—turning suddenly to* COOK). And take this woman here! Stand up, please! Up! Let me look at you!

COOK *(also looking at her as though mesmerized).* Eh? *(She rises.)*

ROSA. Now, this woman I *might* use—at a pinch!

A down-and-out in a dockside-pub scene, or a drunken old flower-woman in a fog. She's *a* type, but not *the* type ! Oh dear, no ! (*To* COOK.) Sit down, please !

COOK (*sitting very abruptly*). Ho !

ROSA. You see, Janet, how maddeningly difficult it all is ! This needle in a haystack that I've *got* to find ! Where is she ? Where ? Echo answers with that one word—" *Where ?* "

JANET. Echo's lucky to get even one word in, if you ask me.

ROSA. What, dear ?

JANET. Nothing.

ROSA. Of course, it's only a small part, but it's the most tense and vital moment of the whole film ! In fact, it's the most stupendous moment in any film I've ever done ! Just try to imagine the situation, dear ! The scene's as it might be in this very room, and here they are, waiting, holding their breaths, wondering what's going to happen next, when, suddenly, the door (*pointing to the area-door*), *that* door, begins slowly to open, and—and *she* comes in ! The *woman* !

(*And lo ! as she utters the last word, the area door does open, revealing* MRS. LOCKETT, *carrying her empty pail. Closing the door quietly behind her, she starts to drift towards the kitchen, looking neither to right nor to left. Her appearance, insignificant though it be, has had an instantaneous effect upon* MISS ROSA ROSARIO, *causing her to gasp, then freeze into a sudden silence, as she follows with her eyes the drab and undramatic figure. And then :*)

(*In an awestricken whisper.*) Who is she ? (*Louder.*) Janet ! That woman ! Who is she ?

JANET. What ?

(MRS. LOCKETT *has disappeared into the kitchen.*)

ROSA (*starting to hurry towards the kitchen*). You—you with the bucket !—come here, please !—quickly !—I want you !——

(MRS. LOCKETT *reappears in the doorway.*)

MRS. LOCKETT (*timidly*). Was someone a'calling of me, please ?

ROSA (*to her—her excitement increasing*). Stand there ! Don't move ! Let me look at you ! (*Stepping back, the better to study her—then, clasping her hands ecstatically.*) But, Janet—she's *it* ! She's absolutely *it* !—Why, she's what I've been searching for all over London ! (*She takes another step back.*) Oh, *yes* ! Janet, I've found her at *last* !

(MRS. LOCKETT *stares at* ROSA *and then, suddenly, drops the bucket with a clatter, and rushes to* JANET.)

MRS. LOCKETT (*panic-stricken*). Oh, don't let 'er take me, Missis !—If it's that bit o' beef-dripping as I took 'ome with me the other day—I didn't mean it to be real stealing. Missis, I didn't mean it to be real stealing !

JANET. Mrs. Lockett ! for heaven's sake, calm yourself !

MRS. LOCKETT. She's from the p'lice ! She's come to take me away ! Oh, Missis !

JANET (*louder*). She is *not* from the police, you silly woman.

MRS. LOCKETT (*checked—looking at* JANET, *then at* ROSA, *then at* JANET *again*). If she's not from the p'lice—what can she want with me ?

ROSA (*rapturously*). Janet ! Janet, she's *wonderful* ! She's *superb* ! She's *everything* we ever *dared* to hope for—and more ! I've a contract-form in my bag ! I've been carrying it about with me for weeks, just in case ! She must sign it before she leaves this room ! She must ! (*To* MRS. LOCKETT.) Oh—oh, you darling !

MRS. LOCKETT. Eh ?

ROSA (*getting to business at once—opening her hand-bag—speaking very rapidly*). Now, listen very carefully : you're to come to the Studio at nine o'clock to-morrow morning. (*Whisking a card from her bag—thrusting it into* MRS. LOCKETT's *hand.*) There's the address ! And you're to come in the clothes you're wearing now, mind ! No dolling yourself up in your

Sunday best! Exactly as you are now! We'll explain everything to you, and we'll be able to start shooting at once!

MRS. LOCKETT (*the look of fear returning*). Shooting, Missis?

ROSA. We'll need you every morning for a fortnight—and we'll pay you a hundred pounds!

MRS. LOCKETT (*bewildered*). Eh——?

ROSA. On condition that you sign the contract now! (*Grasping her by the arm—dragging her round to the back of the table.*) Sit down! Sit down! (*She thrusts the stupefied woman into the chair at the back of the table.*) Now, where's the contract-form? Oh, Janet, this is too *wonderful*! (*She whips the form from her bag, and slams it down on the table in front of* MRS. LOCKETT.) And here's a pen! (*She snatches a fountain pen from her bag, and thrusts it into* MRS. LOCKETT's *hand.*) See, that's where you sign—that space, there!

MRS. LOCKETT. But—I don't know what it's all about, Missis.

ROSA. Good heavens! I've told you, haven't I? I want you to act in a film.

MRS. LOCKETT. In a film? Me?

ROSA (*impatiently*). Yes! Yes! Now, don't let's waste any more time! Sign where I told you! (*Going to* JANET.) Darling, I can't tell you what a relief this is to me! I just can't *tell* you! Monty will be wild with joy!

IRIS (*faintly—as she sees her dreams lying in the dust*). Oh, Cook!

JANET (*tartly—her nerves on edge*). Meanwhile, I lose my perfectly good charwoman!

ROSA. In the cause of Art, dear, remember.

JANET. Indeed!

IRIS (*as before*). Oh, Cook! (*Suddenly springing up from the sofa—with a sob.*) Oh!—Oh, I can't bear it!—It isn't fair!—It isn't fair!—I——

(*With her apron to her eyes, she rushes blindly across to the kitchen door, and out.*)

JANET (*startled*). Iris! Cook, what's the matter with Iris? Is she ill?

COOK. No, Madam—she's just a bit upset, that's all.

JANET. Upset? But—— (*Breaking off as she notices* IVY'S *attitude*.) Ivy! Why are you sitting there like that?

COOK (*hastily*). Ivy, get off that pouffe this instant-minute, and pull your stockings up, d'you hear?

IVY (*rising*). I was only being deaf and dumb, like you said.

JANET. What on earth is she talking about?

COOK. Don't be so silly, Ivy! (*To* JANET.) She's like this some days. It's just a mood.

JANET. Mood, indeed! (*To* IVY.) Run along after Iris, you silly girl, and see if she's all right.

IVY. Yes, Madam.

(*She hurries out.*)

JANET (*to* ROSA). They're behaving very oddly. I can't think what's wrong with them!

ROSA. Nothing's wrong at all, dear! My search is ended, and everything's gloriously, dazzlingly right! Oh, I'm so happy!

JANET (*coldly*). How nice for you.

ROSA (*briskly—returning to* MRS. LOCKETT). Now then—— Why, but you haven't signed it!

(MRS. LOCKETT *has been staring down at the sheet of paper, and now the pen falls from her fingers to the table.*)

MRS. LOCKETT. No, and I'm not going to, neither·

ROSA. My good woman!

MRS. LOCKETT. It isn't no use you trying to persuade me, Missis, for I won't do it. I'm not going to mess about with no film, not for no one.

ROSA. Don't be silly!

MRS. LOCKETT (*stubbornly*). Silly I may be. But I'm not going to be acting in no film.

ROSA. But—a hundred pounds, woman—think!

MRS. LOCKETT. I've thought! I'm all right as I am. I'm sorry as 'ow I can't oblige, Missis, but I'm all right as I am, and I'm not going to change, I'm not.

ROSA (*baffled*). This is ridiculous! (*To* JANET—*helplessly.*) Janet, can't you make her see sense?

JANET. Why should I try? She's a very good charwoman.

ROSA. I don't think that's very friendly of you, darling.

JANET (*snapping*). I can't help that!

ROSA (*shrilly*). Janet, is it quite necessary for you to adopt this tone?

JANET. Yes, if it relieves my feelings! I've had a thoroughly tiresome afternoon, after listening to your maddening chatter about your rotten film!— and I can bear no more!

ROSA. *What?*

JANET. On top of which, you deliberately try to filch my charwoman from under my very nose!

ROSA. Oh! This is too much!

JANET. You're quite right! It is—far too much! I shall go to my room and lie down—and will you kindly control the impulse to slam the door when you leave!

(*She sweeps out.* ROSA *stands quite still for a second, seething. Then :*)

ROSA. Oh! (*And again—even more explosively.*) Oh ! ! ! ! !

(*She seethes for a further second or two, then she snatches the pen and paper from the table, and strides furiously from the room. There is a short, stunned silence after her cyclonic departure. Then :*)

COOK (*in awestricken tones*). Mrs. Lockett ! . . . Mrs. Lockett, why—whatever can you be <u>thinking</u> of? *One hundred pounds!*

MRS. LOCKETT (*turning her head slowly—looking at her—wanly*). I know . . . Oh, what a godsend it would 'ave been to me . . . One 'undred pounds . . . No more slaving and scraping . . . Eh dear!

Cook. But—but whatever made you—— *(Speech fails her.)*

Mrs. Lockett. It . . . it were when she asked me to write me name. . . . I'd 'ave been that ashamed for a lady like 'er to know . . . I weren't never taught 'ow to write. . . . *(A very short pause, then she rises slowly—drifting towards the kitchen.)* I 'aven't never thought so much of eddication up to now . . . but, seemingly, there's something in it, after all. *(She stoops and picks up the pail—pausing for a moment in the doorway.)* Eh, well, it's no use fretting. . . .

She goes. Cook remains seated in her chair, staring towards the open doorway. And then, slowly, wonderingly, she shakes her head from side to side. And as she does so—

The Curtain falls.